For Our Family
and Friends

About the Authors

Onkaar is a 10 year old happy and confident boy. He loves exploring nature and the world around us. He finds different ways to let nature shine into his life!

Avneet is an 8 year old calm and inquisitive girl who loves connecting with nature to relax. She wants everyone to open their eyes and really see the wonderful world around us!

Onkaar and Avneet have each won awards for their writing and are excited to share their love for nature and creativity with young people across the world!

"We want to help young people connect with nature and see their world differently.

It will help you to discover the beauty and magic inside you and around you!"

Avneet & Onkaar

Have you got this?

Onkaar is the Author of "A Kids View on Confidence" which he wrote for young people to build their confidence through fun activities.

Onkaar supports several charities. He donated the proceeds from this book to Save The Children charity.

So together we are making the world a better place for young people!

★★★★★

Onkaar is also Ambassador of Botanic Shed, and he delivers workshops to young people to encourage wellbeing through nature.

This book is not for profit.

Acknowledgements

We want to thank our Mummy and Daddy for giving us the gift of life!

Our parents have always helped us to explore and learn new lessons on our journey through life. We call it the 'game of life' and we are here to enjoy it.

We also want to thank each other for being brilliant companions as brother and sister. Sometimes we bicker but we always make each other think about things in life.

We have a special thanks to Lara Cowan, Founder of Botanic Shed, who works hard to help people learn about the power of connecting with nature.

We hope you enjoy this book!

Onkaar & Avneet

Take a quiet walk with Mother Nature.

It will nurture your mind, body and soul.

Anthony Douglas Williams

Foreword

Nature is our greatest teacher and the most compassionate friend we could wish for. Just think, when an apple tree produces her fruits, she expects nothing back in return but shares her delicious fruit with everyone!

Nature is also our home and sanctuary. We need the support of Mother Nature and she needs our support too. Over the years, we haven't done enough to protect the planet for our children's future, and they deserve to play a meaningful role in changing attitudes towards our relationship with nature.

Onkaar and Avneet have already made their mark in this way. This book is a wonderful companion and guide for children as they grow and learn about ways to nurture Mother Earth. When Botanic Shed was launched, part of our vision was to change the lives of children and young people, so we donate a percentage of our profits to Jamie's Farm, a charity that offers children a programme of "family, farming and therapy".

When I met Onkaar I was so impressed with his first book called "A Kid's View on Confidence" and his passion to selflessly help other children that I invited him to be an Ambassador for Botanic Shed. Our aim is to help families, children and young adults flourish socially and cognitively by teaching them to observe and understand nature's processes and bring nature connection into their daily lives.

Among the collection of activities and events at Botanic Shed, the garden therapy sessions are those closest to my heart because it is so clear that nature connection through gardening is a true salvation for our soul and for society. The activities in this book encourage children to go outdoors, immerse themselves in nature, observe the processes of nature and engage in mindful activities. There is new evidence that our minds thrive when we do this. Exposure to nature can restore the negative effects that media and technology has on cognitive function. For instance you could experience up to 50% boost in creativity after spending a few days steeped in nature.

So take this book away as a family for a few days on a nature holiday to strengthen your whole health now and into the future. Flick through the book and you will find a variety of ideas including ways to look after the environment. Look for a fantastic chapter called Space that starts with the quote 'Reach for the Stars', and go on a tree hunt to see if you can find one that is so old, it is called a living fossil. Enjoy it all!

This book is a wonderful guide to help children and their families along their nature connection journey.

Lara Cowan
Founder of Botanic Shed
Natural Health Club

BOTANIC SHED
SCHOOL OF NATURE

Contents

If you truly love nature, you will find beauty everywhere

Laura Ingalls Wilder

Introducing Sticky

Sticky will help you

You will love all the fun activities in this book!

For some activities, Sticky will guide you through and for some you may need an adult helper too.

This book will certainly get you seeing and thinking about the nature and the wonderful world around us in a new and exciting way.

The activities are designed to get you thinking and help you get involved to explore the world around you. So roll up your sleeves and get stuck in!

You can also use this book as part of your wellbeing journey so that you grow and understand more about yourself as you connect with Mother Nature.

Connect with Nature

The air we breath, the water we drink and the ground we walk on are all little miracles of nature. Every season that we experience is the delicate display of nature at work.

Nature is the foundation of our existence.

Everywhere we look nature has played a part. However nature is not only around us, it is inside us too. So when you connect with nature around you, it will help you to connect with your inner self!

Lots of clever scientists have done research about how nature is good for our body and mind, and they are right.

Why it helps:

Physical Health

When we are outdoors and connecting with nature around us, we are being active, So our body is getting exercise. Everytime we exercise, our body gets stronger and healthier.

Mental health and Wellbeing (Happiness!)

Being out and about releases lots of positive messages from your brain to other parts of your body. It also releases 'happy' hormones called endorphins which help us to feel relaxed and calm.

This book will help you to connect with nature.

It is packed with fun activities which will get you outside and perhaps a little bit muddy (but that is part of the fun!). You must have an adult with you when you are doing the activities because they are responsible and need to make sure that you are safe.

Also remember to wash your hands after the activities (and sometimes you might need to change your muddy clothes).

With every activity you will feel the power of nature around you. Look around you at the colours, listen to the sounds, smell the air and feel the positivity of nature pulse through you.

Let nature shine into your life!

Chapter 1

Humans & Habitats

Without habitat, there is no wildlife

Wildlife Habitat Canada

Habitats

A habitat is where an animal or plant lives. Their habitat is their home. It provides them with a suitable space to live and grow. It provides shelter, food and water.

There are lots of different types of habitat across the world. For example, there are deserts, forests, grasslands, lakes, mountains, ponds and loads more.

Each different type of habitat has different types of animals or plants living there. Within the habitat, the animals and plants all interact and live together in healthy balance. This is called an ecosystem.

Habitats and ecosystems can be big, like the ocean, or small, like a tree or bush in your garden.

Think of a habitat and write down all the animals and plants which live there

Reflect and feel inside you nature's...

Poetry Power

...as you write an Acrostic Poem

H

A

B

I

T

A

T

How to make your own...

Wild Patch

...to make a new habitat in your garden

A habitat is the natural home or environment of an animal or a plant. It is easy to attract new wildlife into your garden by creating a small 'wild patch' which will make a new mini habitat.

All you need is a meter or two of a grassy area. Let the grass there grow longer. This is your wild patch, so leave it to grow wild!

Things you could add to your wild patch:

- Trees
- Shrubs
- Flowers
- Herbs
- Soil patch
- Ivy
- Bamboo sticks

You will start to notice new bugs and insects which you may not have spotted in your garden before.

So remember to regularly check on your wild patch to see what is growing there.

Different types of Habitat

Your wild patch will be a new habitat for lots of different little creatures. Here are some examples of different habitats for different creatures.

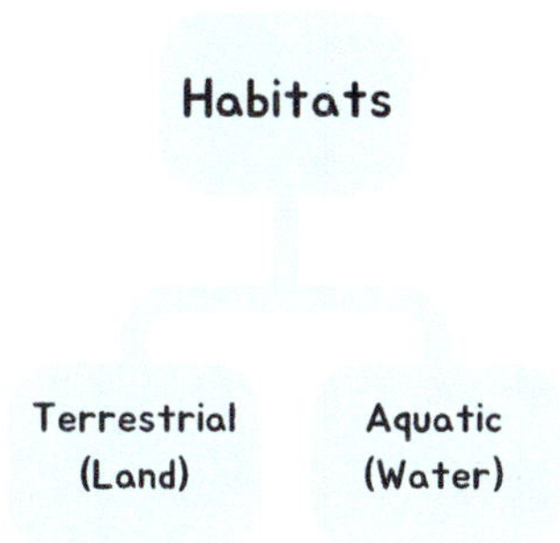

Terrestrial habitats

These are land based habitats which include grassland (like your wild patch), woodland, deserts, rainforests and mountains. They are the home for billions of creatures all over our planet.

Aquatic habitats

These are water based habitats which include ponds, oceans and coral reefs. A ginormous number of creatures live under in water and especially under the sea.

Supporting different habitats is important so that different animals and plants can survive.

How to make your own...

Mini Stone Wall

...to attract minibeasts to your garden

You will need:

- Trowel
- Different sizes of stones
- Plants
- Shrubs
- Peat-free compost
- A sunny/shady place for your wall

1. Choose a suitable area to build your mini stone wall.
2. With your trowel, dig a small ditch for the first layer of stones. Put down the larger and more flat stones for the first layer.
3. Gradually pile the rocks one on the other. Keep the base wider. Make the layers less wide as you increase the height of layers. This will make it more stable.
4. Use the compost in between the stones to help hold them together. If you want to add herbs and shrubs to your wall, you can slip them into the cracks and gaps in your wall.

Your stone wall will become home to lots of minibeasts. Tick the minibeasts which you see living in there.

☐ 

Spider

☐ 

Centipede

☐ 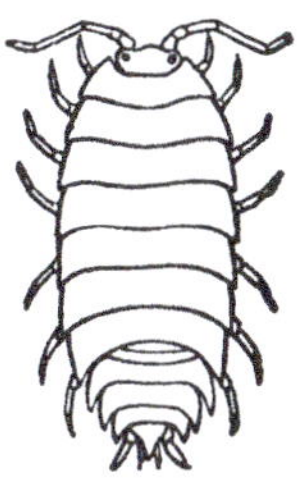

Woodlouse

☐ 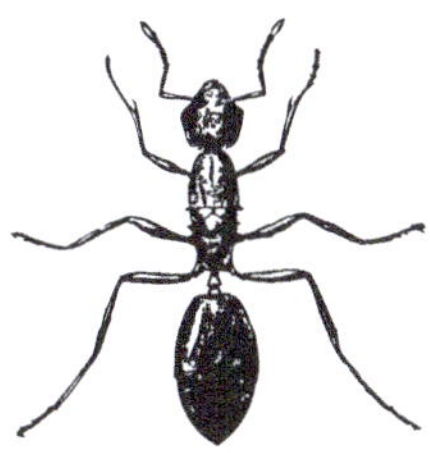

Ant

Remember to regularly check on your mini stone wall and check out the minibeasts living there. Try not to disturb them...after all it is their home!

How to make your own...

Beetle Bucket

...to give beetles a new home

You will need:

- A bucket
- A small craft knife
- Stones
- Bark chips
- Leaves
- Soil
- A spade

Top Tips:

If you would rather not use plastic, you can dig a small hole in the ground and make this directly in there.

Check regularly on your beetle bucket to make sure the minibeasts have a nice new home!

1. Cut circular holes (around 3 cm wide) in the sides and bottom of the bucket with the craft knife. This will be how beetles to enter and exit.

2. Dig a hole a bit larger than your bucket and push it firmly into the ground.

3. Place some large stones at the bottom of the bucket, then place upright some small logs on top.

4. Fill the rest of the bucket with leaves and wood chips. Save some space at the top to fill with soil from the ground.

5. Place some soil and leaves on top so that the beetles are tempted to enter.

Tick which Beetles you spot in your battle bucket.

☐ 

Sexton Beetle

☐ 

Ladybird

☐ 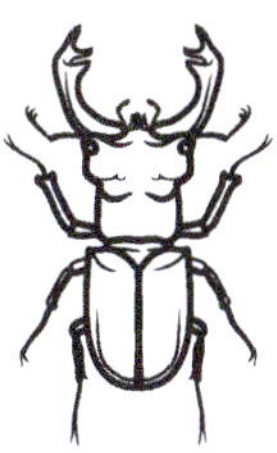

Lesser stag beetle

☐ 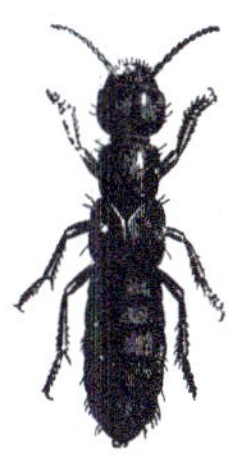

Devils Coach Horse

How to make a ...

Hedgehog Home

...a fun way to support our hedgehog population

It is good to support hedgehogs because they feed on other small creatures that live in the soil. So a drop in hedgehog population indicates a drop in the quality of our soil environment and the health of the natural world. Hedgehogs hibernate over the winter and a hedgehog home can support them.

You will need:

- A medium sized wood or plastic box
- Stanley Knife
- Leaf Litter
- Straw or dry grass
- Heavy cardboard
- Twigs or dry leaves

1. Cut two air holes in the side of the box.
2. Cut a 15cm by 15cm entrance.
3. Place some leaf litter inside and top with dry grass or straw.
4. Put your heavy cardboard on top and cover with twigs and dry leaves.

Tips For your hedgehog home

- Make sure your home is well insulated
- Make sure it has comfy bedding
- Make sure the hedgehog has space

How was it building the hedgehog home? Reflect and write here

How to make a...

Mini Pond

...to support a pond habitat

You will need:

- A large container that can hold water
- Some gravel and rocks
- Some small pond plants (e.g watercress)

1. Dig a hold into the ground, make sure it is a bit larger than the container.
2. Place the container inside.
3. Place some stones around it for edging.
4. Put in some gravel to hold the pond plants still.
5. Place the pond plants inside the container and secure them with the stones.
6. Use larger stones to trail into the pond, to make it easier for animals like frogs to get in and out.
7. Fill your pond with rainwater.

Which are frogs? Colour the frogs in

Draw your own Frog here

Chapter 2

Spectacular Space

Laugh often,
Dream big
&
Reach for the
stars

Don Williams Jr

Space

Space is ENORMOUS!

It is so big that it can be tricky to imagine its size and all the things that are out there. So Sticky will help you out here.

UNIVERSE

↓

GALAXY

↓

SOLAR SYSTEM

OUR SOLAR SYSTEM

MERCURY

Mercury is the closest planet to the Sun and the smallest in our solar system

VENUS

On Venus one day is longer than one day on Earth

EARTH

Earth is the 3rd planet from the Sun and is the only place in the known universe which hosts life

MARS

Mars has two moons and is named after the Roman God of war. It is also known as the 'Red Planet'

JUPITER

Jupiter is massive and it can fit three Earth-sized planets in it! But it spins the fastest. The Great Red Spot is a gigantic storm site

SATURN

Saturn is not the only planet with rings, but it has the most beautiful ones! The rings are made of chunks of ice and rock

URANUS

Uranus is the 7th planet from the Sun and it is an ice giant. Uranus is unique in because it rotates on its side

NEPTUNE

Neptune is the furthest from the Sun and takes about 165 Earth years to orbit the Sun

DID YOU KNOW:
FROM 2006 PLUTO WAS NO LONGER CONSIDERED A PLANET

Not to Scale!!

How to make a...

Space mobile

...a fun and easy way!

You will need:

- 2 sheets of white card
- 1 sheet of black card
- Pencil
- Scissors
- Coloured Paint
- Tape
- Paint Brushes
- A pin
- Thread

1. With your pencil, draw 8 circles on the white card for the planets. Make a sun too if you like.
2. Cut the circles out with scissors.
3. Using the paint and brushes paint your circles. Make different patterns and textures with your brush.
4. Cut a large circle from your black card, then mark the centre and, with a pin, make small holes this is where you planets will hang.
5. Make a hole at the top of each planet and thread a piece of thread through the hole.
6. Finally push the loose end of your thread through a hole in the black card and tie a knot.

Here are some painting top tips to make your space mobile look even more life like!

Mercury has a rocky surface with craters a bit like our moon.

Venus has a thick atmospheric layer so you can make the planet look hazy by blending your paint colours.

The surface of Earth is over 70% water so use blue shades for this and use green paints for all of the land.

Mars has a very rusty red coloured surface with darker parts, so use a range of light and dark shades.

Jupiter has the Great Red Spot, which is a huge storm system so you can add a red dot there.

Saturn has faint banding across the surface and the stunning rings.

Uranus and Neptune both have faint banding on their surface too so you could add some stripes of purple and blue.

If you made a Sun, paint some sunspots and add an orange texture.

Solar System Trivia

This Solar System trivia will test your knowledge about space. Have a go with all of the questions to see what you remember from the last few pages. Have fun!

Which planet is furthest away from the Sun?

Neptune Uranus Mars Earth

Which is the closest planet to the Sun?

Jupiter Earth Mercury Uranus

The planet named after the Roman god of war is...

Venus Earth Mars Saturn

Which is the fastest spinning planet in our Solar System?

Mars Jupiter Mercury Uranus

Excellent effort!

How did you find this trivia?

Solar System Word search

Have a go at completing this Solar System word search.
Find the words in the list on the word search.
Good Luck!

S	M	I	L	K	Y	W	A	Y	A	S	A	C	T
S	U	O	C	N	S	N	N	K	T	H	R	T	J
R	O	U	S	T	A	R	A	I	T	M	T	I	U
U	P	E	A	E	S	L	S	R	P	S	U	P	P
A	Y	A	T	L	U	M	A	E	S	N	E	C	I
E	E	I	U	A	N	E	Y	N	U	I	O	A	T
N	T	A	R	I	E	R	S	N	N	M	Y	M	E
E	P	U	N	T	V	A	U	A	E	S	A	C	R
P	U	Y	P	S	E	R	R	T	W	R	O	W	S
T	J	N	T	R	T	R	A	E	O	U	I	R	E
U	M	N	S	N	R	R	A	R	S	T	A	N	J
N	T	N	P	L	A	N	E	T	E	M	A	Y	A
E	P	N	T	S	H	E	C	T	T	H	W	K	I
C	O	N	S	T	E	L	L	A	T	I	O	N	S

Planet	Star	Mars
Jupiter	Neptune	Sun
Venus	MilkyWay	Saturn
Comet	Earth	Constellations

I NEED SOME SPACE!

Stop for a moment.

Give yourself some space.

Look into the dark night sky one evening.

Take in what you see.
Breathe in the air and
slowly breathe out.

Look at the stars and simply RELAX.

DREAM BIG

REACH FOR THE STARS

Dream big and aim for the stars!

It is good to think about your dreams and ambition in life. Take pride in things that you enjoy doing. We all love doing different things and so our dreams and goals will be different too.

Be proud of who you are and what you want to become!

You could dream about things like:

- To have a certain job
- To get a certain grade
- To travel somewhere

Whatever your dream is, nobody can take it away from you. It belongs to you, and when you succeed you will be double happy!

IT'S TIME TO DREAM...

Write your dreams and
hopes for the future here

PHASES OF THE MOON

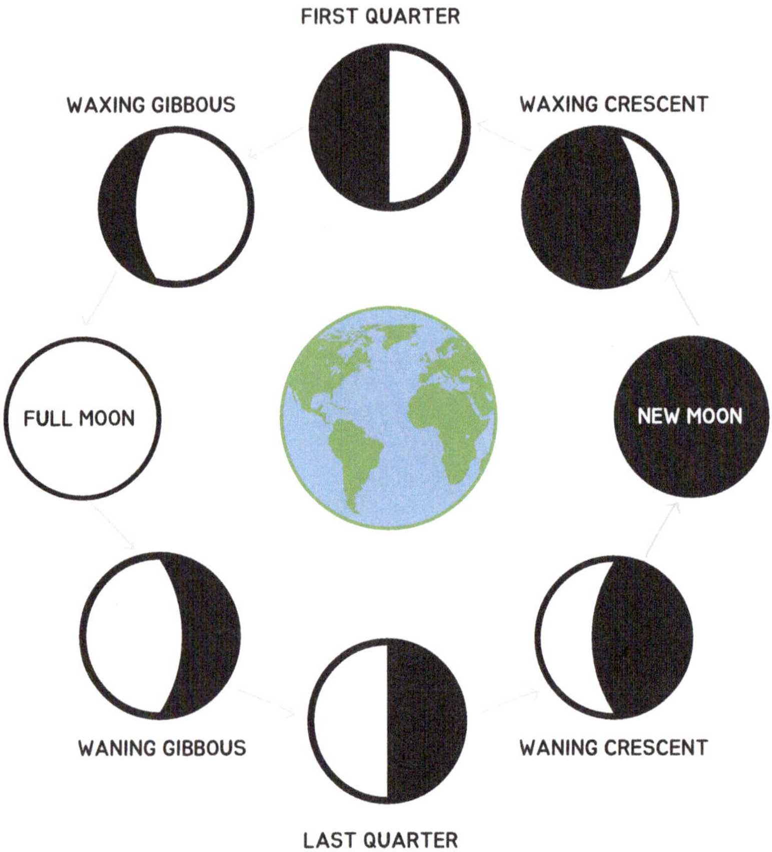

When you look up at the night sky before you go to bed you may see the moon. Do you notice the different shapes of the moon? These are the phases of the moon and they are made by the Earth casting a shadow on the moon.

WHAT MOON PHASE IS IT?

Now that you know what the phases of the moon look like, have a go at identifying them for yourself.

On this calendar write the month, and every day in the boxes draw the phase for the moon that you see.

Month ______________

Sleepy Head

Sleep is when you recharge. Your brilliant body grows and repairs itself while you sleep which makes you stronger and feel fresh.

It is important to have a good amount of sleep as your body needs time to repair and reset.

Benefits of Sleeping

Healthier heart

Sleeping helps your heart and blood pressure. When we sleep our body is relaxed and resting so our heart rate and blood pressure are not high like they are when we are awake and active.

Better immune system

Sleeping helps your body to have a strong and well balanced immune defence that fights illnesses and keeps you well.

Sharper brain and better memory

Sleeping helps your brain to recharge. It also helps to consolidate your memory which is key for learning new things.

Happier and good mood

Sleeping helps your body and mind to feel good and feel happy. Scientist say that poor sleep can lead to stress and anger. So chill out and sleep!

Sticky has poor sleep hygiene

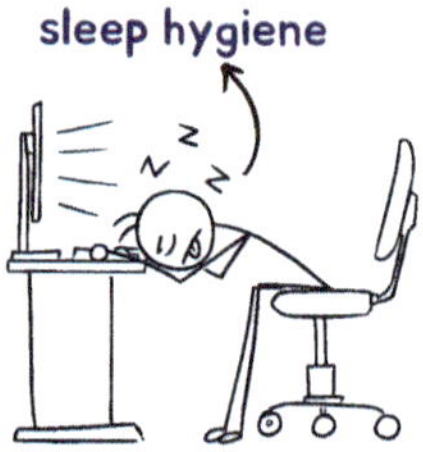

Are you getting enough sleep?

Check if you are getting enough hours of sleep each night...and check if the adults around you are too!

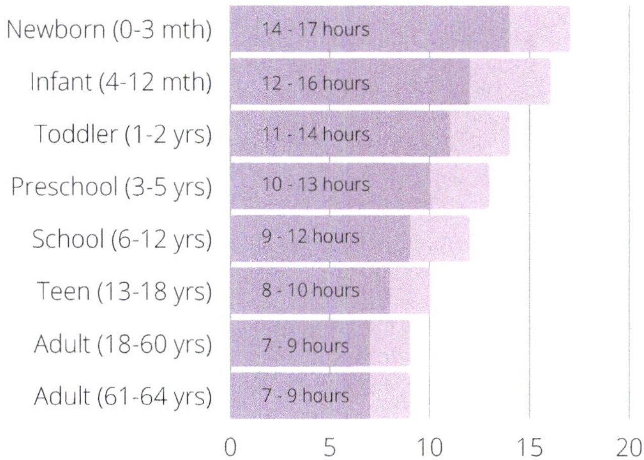

Top tips to get better sleep

Good sleep habits (sleep hygiene) help us to sleep. Here are some tips to help improve your sleep hygiene and get a good night of rest.

- **Be consistent with your sleep time each night and try to wake up at the same time each morning (including on weekends!)**
- **Make sure your bedroom is quiet, relaxing and a comfortable temperature.**
- **Turn off bright lights and remove electronic devices, such as TVs, computers, and smart phones, from your bedroom.**

Planet Earth

Our planet Earth is precious to us.

It is the only habitable (we can live on) planet in the solar system because of the land, water and air balance it has. Sometimes people forget how lucky we are to have such an amazing planet and that Mother Nature is the reason we survive!

As humans we have a responsibility to look after Earth. If we all take one small step towards helping our planet, then together we will make a massive difference.

Global warming is something we can tackle together by being smarter about things we recycle, the type of energy we use and by wasting less.

Have a think about a simple change you could make to help our planet.

DID YOU KNOW?

The oxygen we breath comes from LEAVES on the trees around us. A special process called 'photosynthesis' makes oxygen in the leaf which we can then breath in to survive.

Here are some helpful steps you can take to help planet Earth. Have a think of some more too.

Turn off lights and taps at home so it uses up less electricity and less water is wasted.

Cut down things that get thrown away or wasted, like food or packaging. Reuse items and eat up or compost food rather than waste it.

Separate waste items so that things can be recycled.

Walk, walk, walk and it is healthy.

Chapter 3

Crazy about Clouds

Every cloud has a silver lining

John Milton

Learn about the...

Types of Clouds

...a fun way to learn about clouds!

Clouds are made of little droplets of water. Different clouds tell you different things about the weather. Read on to explore more...

Cirrus Clouds

Cirrus clouds are the highest type of cloud. They are above 18,000 feet. They look like wispy white lines across the sky. Cirrus clouds are made up of ice crystals and they are normally white and predict pleasant weather.

Cirrus clouds predict pleasant weather

Cumulus Clouds

Cumulus means a heap or pile. They are fluffy and tend to be seen on a sunny day. Cumulus clouds look like white candy floss! Most forms of cumulus clouds will not produce any rain or snow. Larger cumulus clouds can produce some rain showers but these are not usually heavy.

Cumulus clouds look like fluffy white candy floss

Look up at the sky. Look for some clouds. Make sure you are calm and relaxed. If you see a cloud try and identify it, then draw it in this box.

Think of a time where you have felt happy or bouncy of have felt as light and as joyful as a cirrus cloud. Picture it in your head and write down the feelings which you felt then.

Stratus Clouds

These are the most common types of cloud in Britain. They are low layers of clouds and tend to block light from the sun. They are found up to 6500 feet from the ground.They can be any shade from white to grey. They often bring rain!

Stratus Clouds often mean rain!

Nimbus Clouds

Nimbus clouds are powerful clouds. You don't want to get stuck in the heavy rain or snow it produces! Nimbus is a word which can be added to the other types of clouds, e.g. cumulonimbus. They are often grey and sometimes reach a very dark grey!

You do not want to get stuck in one of these downpours!

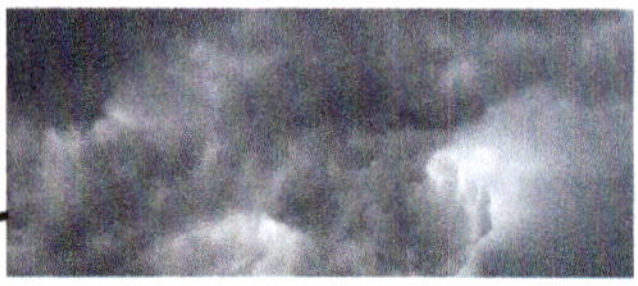

Cumulonimbus Clouds

Cumulonimbus are storm clouds. They can reach huge sizes. The rain they produce comes suddenly and ferociously. They can also produce snow or hailstones and cause thunder and lightning storms. Again, keep inside when they are around!

These are very powerful clouds!

Think of a time where you have sad or angry or worried or upset a bit like a cumulonimbus cloud. Picture it in your head and write down the feelings that you felt then.

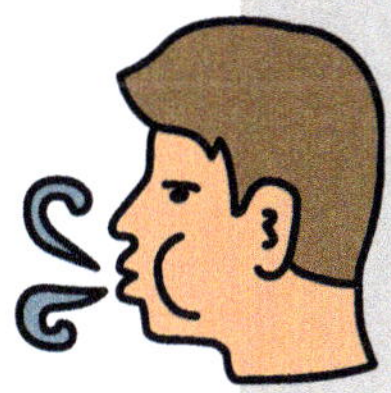

Now, take a moment to blow away those feelings. Breath in and feel the air fill up your lungs, then blow out long and hard. Feel your power and blow away any dark clouds or negative feelings like upset, worry or anger.

Remember, in the same way that storm clouds pass, negative feelings pass too.

Sticky reminds us that to make a rainbow you need rain, and that rain, or a bad day, will help you to be grateful for the good brighter days. So be positive and enjoy the rainbow!

How to make your own pine cone...

Bird Feeder

...a simple way attract birds to your garden

You will need:

- Chopped nuts
- Hard cooking fat
- Pine cone or yoghurt pot
- String
- Bird seeds
- Dry cooked rice
- Grated cheese
- Dried fruit

1. Put all of the dry ingredients into a bowl
2. Add the cooking fat and mix it well
3. Coat the pine cone in the mix or fill your pot with it
4. Hang your bird feeders with string and watch for birds!

Write down the birds you see!

Birds you may see...

Robin

Blue Tit

House sparrow

Goldfinch

Starling

Great Tit

Seeds Birds Like:

- Flaked maize
- Sunflower seeds
- Peanut granules
- Sunflower kernels
- Corn

Birds

In the wild there are lots of different species of bird and they can sometimes be hard to identify.

Birds of Prey

Kestrel

Peregrine Falcon

Bald Eagle

Garden Birds

Robin

Blue-Tit

House Sparrow

Did you know?

Eagles and many other birds of prey can see four to five times better than a human? A bald eagle could spot a rabbit from three miles away!

Migration

Many birds migrate (travel) from a colder climate to a warmer climate. Have a go finding where these birds migrate to. Draw lines to the place they go. Have fun!

Thrush

Swift

Osprey

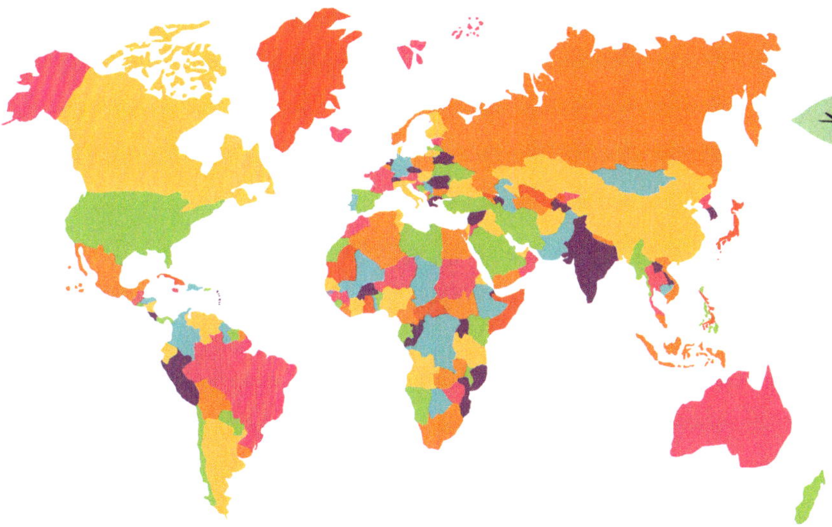

Thrush: Belgium and northern Spain. Swift: Africa. Osprey: West Africa

How to make your own...

Bird House

...a simple way to attract birds to your garden

You will need:

- Milk carton
- Chopstick or perch
- Nontoxic felt pens or pencils
- Twine

1. Choose your desired empty milk carton, this will be the main "room" of your house.

2. Cut a hole with a diameter of 5cm. This will be the bird entrance.

3. With some scissors make a hole and push your chopstick through about 1.5 inches from the bottom. This will be the perch.

4. Decorate you bird house! Maybe add a small roof or draw with pens.

5. Loop some twine over the top and hang on a branch for the birds.

Tops Tips for your Bird House:

- If your bird house is blowing too much, then weigh it down with a few stones and pebbles.
- Make sure you have hooked your bird house on a strong branch - you do not want it falling off!
- Make sure your perch is tightly fitted otherwise it may break off!

After you have hung your feeders keep an eye on it and look out for any birds. You might see some of these.

☐ 

Blue - Tit

☐ 

Sparrow

☐ 

Robin

☐ 

Jay

Chapter 4

Look at Leaves

Learn character

from trees,

values from roots

and

change from leaves

Tasneern Harneed

How to do...

Leaf Identification

...a fun way to identify leaves

When you see a leaf on the floor it is always nice to know which tree the leaf has come from. Use these examples to learn the name of some.

Rowan Leaf

Sycamore Leaf

Beech Leaf

Goat Willow Leaf

Horse Chestnut Leaf

Oak Leaf

Draw any other leaves you see here

Cover up the page before with a sheet of paper and label this diagram from memory.

Match the leaf picture to the leaf name. Have fun!

Rowan Leaf

Oak Leaf

Goat Willow Leaf

Beech Leaf

Horse Chestnut Leaf

Sycamore Leaf

Only one type of leaf has been used for this pattern.
Do you know which leaf it is?

Answer:___________________

Answer: Beech

Learn about how some...

Trees keep leaves

...but not all of them can do this

You will have noticed that some trees stay green and keep their green leaves all year round. But, in autumn the leaves on other trees change into beautiful colours and then their leaves fall off.

This is because some trees are Evergreen trees and some trees are Deciduous.

Evergreen Tree	Deciduous Tree
This means the tree will keep its leaves & stay green all year	Deciduous means to "fall off" so the leaves will shed in autumn
Leaves are usually thin and spindle like	Leaves are usually broad and large
Examples: Holly and Conifers like red cedar and pine	Examples: Oak, Elm, Maple

Explore and Reflect

Go outside and look at the trees. What do you see? Look at all the vibrant colours and the different shapes and sizes of all the trees.

Write down a description of what you see and how it makes you feel.

DID YOU KNOW?

Ginkgo biloba is about 350 million years old!

Ginkgo biloba is one of the oldest tree species in the world! It is known as a 'living fossil', because it has been around for millions of years.

Interestingly, many medicines are made from trees, plants and herbs. Even today some people use ginkgo biloba as a medication.

How to grow your own...

Tree

...to support the life of animals and us

You will need:

- A bucket
- Early tree sapling
- A spade
- A bamboo stick
- Compost
- A nice space with good soft ground

1. Take your early tree sapling and carefully remove it from its pot.

2. Submerge the root ball in a bucket of water before planting. Make sure all of the roots are in the water because they can quickly dry out.

3. Dig a hole that is at least double the size of the root ball. Mix topsoil and compost together, these will give nutrition to the tree.

4. Put your tree in the centre of the hole and make sure the roots are gently spread out.

5. Spread and flatten the soil around the roots, and water generously on the soil around the roots.

6. Remember to water your tree regularly to help support the main part of your trees growth.

7. When your tree grows over 1.5 metres, attach a bamboo stick to the side. This will give the tree support to help it stay upright (we all need support sometimes!).

How to make your own...

Leaf Collage

...an excellent way to make art with nature

You will need:

- Dry leaves (collect from the floor not from trees)
- Card or Paper
- Glue
- Scissors -optional

1. Collect your leaves. Make sure they are from the floor. Choose a variety of different colours and different type of leaves.

2. Prepare your leaves by placing them under a book to flatten them and leave them on the side to dry. This is important so your work does not get soggy later.

3. Think of the animal you want to make with your leaf collage. You may need to cut some leaves into shapes.

4. Begin sticking your leaves down until you have made your planned animal.

5. Hole punch the top of your card and thread some string through so you can hang up your nature art collage, or you could frame it.

Chapter 5

Funky Flowers

Every flower
blooms
in it's
own time

Ken Petti

Have a look...

Inside a Flower

...another miracle of nature

Flowers are beautiful, vibrant and essential for the survival of billions of insects.

Insects are attracted to the bright colour, strong smell and sweet nectar of flowers. Look at this diagram to learn about what is inside a flower.

There are approximately 369,000 species of flowering plants in the world.
That is a lot!

Help Sticky to name some flowers...

Rose, Lilly, Tulip, Orchid, Gerbera, Iris, Freesia, Carnation, Hyacinth, Bluebell, Chrysanthemum, Snowdrop, Daffodil, Peony, Poppy, Sunflower, Geranium........

What does each part of a flower do?

Each part of the flower has a special role.

Stem - anchors the flower plant to the ground

Petal - attracts the insects (pollinators)

Anther - makes male cells called pollen

Filament - tube connecting to the anther

Stigma - sticky so it can collect pollen

Style - tube connecting to the stigma

Ovary - makes the female cells

Sepal - protects the unopened flower

Cover over the previous page with a sheet of paper and label what you can remember about the cut through (cross-section) a flower.

How to make...

Seed Bombs

...a fun way to plant flowers

You will need:

- Large bowl
- Seeds
- Water
- Powdered clay or clay soil
- Compost (peat free)

1. Get your large bowl and put in 1 cup of seeds
2. Mix the seeds with 5 cups of peat-free compost and 2-3 cups of clay powder (or clay soil if you have it).
3. Add in small amounts of water slowly and mix it with your hands until everything sticks together.
4. Using your hands, roll the mixture into balls.
5. Leave the balls in a sunny spot to dry for 20 minutes
6. Throw your seed balls (bombs!) at parts of the garden where you want them to grow. Water them and wait to see what grows!

Here are some seeds you could put in your seed bomb:

- Sunflower
- Bulbous Buttercup
- Chamomile
- Red Clover
- Wild Thyme
- Poppy
- Marigold

After 6-12 weeks your garden will have burst into colour as the flowers from your seed bomb bloom.

TOP TIPS

Water your seed bomb regularly, especially in hot weather.

Only throw your seed bomb where you have permission to grow flowers. So ask an adult if you are not sure where.

How to help...

Butterflies

...lay their eggs and survive

Everything starts off as an egg. Butterflies lay their eggs on a leaf (host plant). They need a suitable leaf for this and then when the egg hatches into a caterpillar it will enjoy eating the leaves.

Butterflies favourite leaves for laying their eggs on:

- Milkweed
- Lady's smock
- Bird's foot trefoil
- Buckthorn
- Holly
- Ivy

There are 17,500 species of butterfly in the world! With 60 species in the UK!

Monarch Butterfly

Peacock Butterfly

Swallowtail Butterfly

American Painted Lady Butterfly

Butterfly life cycle

Look at this butterfly lifecycle to see the changes which happen before a butterfly is made!

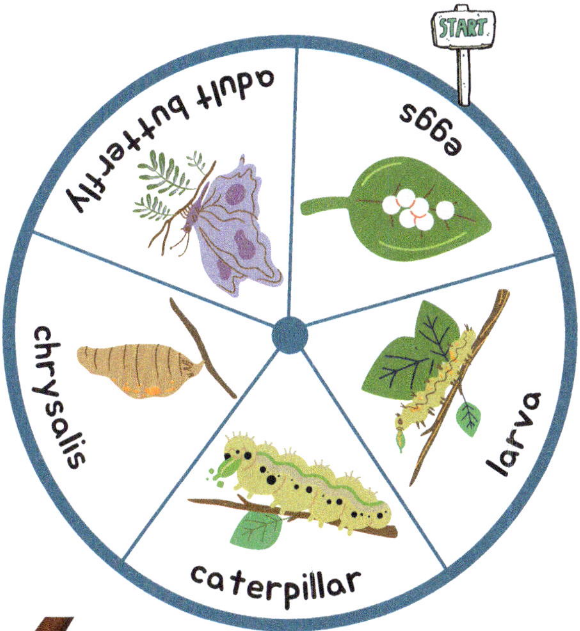

How to make a

Nectar cafe

...to attract bees and butterflies

Bees and butterflies feed on nectar, so they need nectar just like we need food.

While they are feeding on the nectar, they rub against other parts of the flower like the anther and stigma. As they rub, they transfer pollen among different flowers. This is why bees and butterflies are known as 'pollinators'.

Pollination is a very important process for flowers and it is how they reproduce (make more of them).

Draw your favourite flower here. Remember to colour it in with bright colours.

You can plant flowers which attract more bees and butterflies in your garden. Your garden could become a Nectar Cafe!

1. Find a sunny but sheltered spot in your garden
2. Plant your flowers in groups so their scent is stronger and easier for the pollinators to smell.
3. Choose plants which have a long flowering season so that they keep their flowers from early spring until late autumn.
4. Sometimes adding a few herbs can help to attract more insects which is useful.
5. Do not use pesticides on the plants or flowers.

Flowers to plant in a Nectar Cafe

Winter	Spring	Summer
Honeysuckle	Primrose	Heather
Ivy	Lungwort	Lavender
Coneflower	Sweet violet	Wallflower

How to make your own...

Bee Hotel

...it's buzzing good fun!

You will need

- Sturdy outdoor box
- Bamboo Sticks
- String
- Hammer and screws

What to Do

1. Get your sturdy outdoor box
2. Fill your box with pieces of small bamboo sticks
3. Tie your string to the box
4. Hammer a screw onto a wall which gets good sun on it. Try to choose a space which is sheltered from rain. Hook up the string with your bee hotel.

Bee hotel

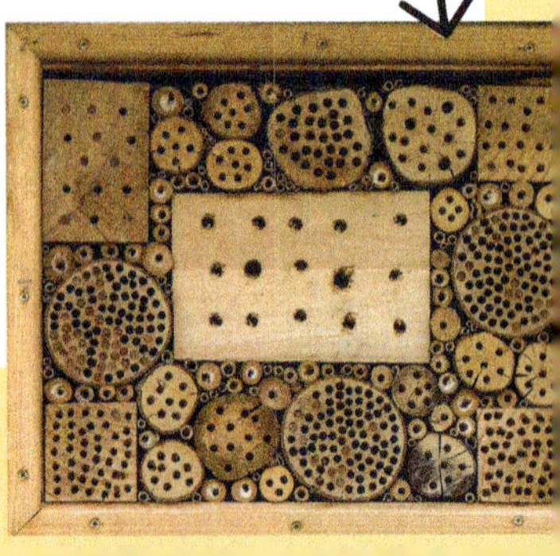

Where do bees go in the winter?

Many people notice that bees seem to disappear during the winter.

Different bee species do different things in winter. There are over 250 bee species in the UK!

Social Bees

Social bees (eg bumblebees and honeybees) focus on their queen and hive during winter. In summer, the queen lays eggs which produce a new generation of queen bees and male bees.

The young queens eat lots of nectar and pollen to build up fat in their bodies so they can hibernate alone underground. Their vital fat stores help them to survive through the winter.

Mason Bees

Mason bees spend winter as pupae. They have a yearly lifecycle that ends after they lay their eggs in autumn.

Solitary Bees

Solitary bees spend their time 'overwintering' which involves them protecting themselves from the cold. They come out again in the spring.

How to make your own...

Lavender Sachet

...to put in your sock drawer!

Lavender has a soothing, floral and fresh smell. You can use a lavender sachet to make your sock drawer smell good, or give as a thoughtful gift.

They are really fun and easy to make.

Top gift idea

You will need:

- Lavender (dried)
- Rice
- Bowl
- Fabric pouch with a tie (or you could sew two pieces of fabric together to make a pouch).

DID YOU KNOW?

Lavender has lots of uses. It has health benefits like improving sleep and it can be used in food and drinks!

This is how to make your lavender pouch:

1. Remove the lavender grains using your fingers and collect them in a bowl

2. Pour some rice into a small bowl

3. Mix the lavender and rice in a 2:1 ratio (so that is like 2 tablespoons of lavender for every 1 tablespoon of rice). Scale it up depending on the size of your pouch.

4. Pour the mixed lavender and rice into your pouch and seal it.

Chapter 6

Valuable Vegetables

Have fruits & vegetables if you want to lead a fruitful life

Unknown

Grow your own...

Vegetable Patch

...fresh vegetables in your back garden

Growing your own vegetables is possible in your garden. It requires planning and commitment but there is a worthwhile harvest at the end of it.

You could get started with some easy to grow vegetables.

Easy to grow vegetables

- Radish
- Carrots
- Peas
- Courgettes
- Squashes
- Potatoes
- Beetroot

DID YOU KNOW?

There are 1097 vegetable species cultivated worldwide.

So no excuses, there is plenty of choice!

Top tips to grow your own Vegetable Patch

1. Choose a suitable place in your garden. Vegetables like to be in the sunshine so choose a patch with at least 5 hours of sunshine per day.

2. Prepare the patch and soil by clearing away any weeds, digging the soil, adding in compost and making the space organised for vegetable sowing.

3. Choose the vegetables which grow best based on the time of year when you sow your seeds.

4. Give enough space between the vegetable so they grow so well. About 20-40cm is sensible distance.

5. Celebrate your harvest! Every year Harvest time reminds us to be grateful for the miracles of Mother Nature.

Learn about...

Food Groups

...to understand how to create a healthy meal

Food groups help us to put all the different foods we have into categories. There are proteins, carbohydrates, dairy, fruit and vegetables.

In a meal you should try to have each one of the food groups on your plate.

Food Group	Example	Benefit
Fruit and Vegetable		Vitamins and nutrients for whole body
Carbohydrate		Energy and fuel
Protein		Repair and growth
Dairy		Strong bones and teeth

Know your foods

For each food, draw a line to the food group which it belongs to. One has been done for you.

Fruit and Veg | Carbohydrate | Protein | Dairy

Food for thought

Think about what you eat and reflect on it.
Which food do you feel you could eat more of?
Which food could you eat less of?

Try these...

Fruit & Vegetable

...activities to work up an appetite

Have fun colouring in the different vegetables and find the hidden fruit!

Which of these is a fruit (not a vegetable)

Healthy Shadows

Complete this activity by drawing lines from the fruit to its shadow. Have fun!

Healthy Bingo

Complete this healthy bingo with your friends and family.

When you eat one of these foods cross it off the grid (in pencil). The first person to get 3 or 4 in a row wins!

How to make your own...

Herb Garden

...and use them in some yummy receipes!

This is a great way to start growing your own food! Most herbs grow well in the garden or on your window sill and they are super tasty too.

You will need:

- Multipurpose peat-free compost
- Small size pots or yoghurt pots (but make some drainage holes)*
- Hand trowel
- Seeds of the herbs you want to grow*
- Plastic bag

*or you could buy potted perennial herbs like mint, oregano, chives, thyme

1. If you are growing from a herb plant, go to step 7. If you are growing from seed, fill your pot with the compost and gently tap it down to remove air pockets and then water it.

2. Scatter a few seeds on the soil surface and cover with a thin layer of compost.

3. Cover the pot with a clear plastic bag to make a mini-greenhouse effect to speed up 'germination' (sprouting of the seedling).

5. After germination, remove the bag and water the compost when dry (about once a week).

6. Once it has grown to 10cm, plant them outside or in a larger pot.

7. Use the trowel to dig a hole just bigger than the size of your small pot.

8. Carefully remove your herb plant from the small pot and place it into the hole

9. Fill with compost and gently pat it so it is stable around the herb plant.

10. Remember to label your herbs so you know what they are when you pick them!

Now wash your hands and take a break...let someone else do the cooking!

Plan Your Meal

Breakfast

Lunch

Dinner

Snacks

Notes

Healthy Food Diary

For the next week, keep a food diary and reflect on how you are doing with hitting 5 portions of fruit and vegetables per day.

Mon

Tue

Wed

Thu

Fri

Sat

Sun

Chapter 7

Super Soils

Soil is Life, Conserve it!

Unknown

What is under your feet?...

Ground

...but there's more than you think!

Look at the ground outside. You will see one flat layer. However, did you know that there are so many layers underneath that?

This picture is a cut (cross-section) through the ground.

These are some of the layers which we are standing on.

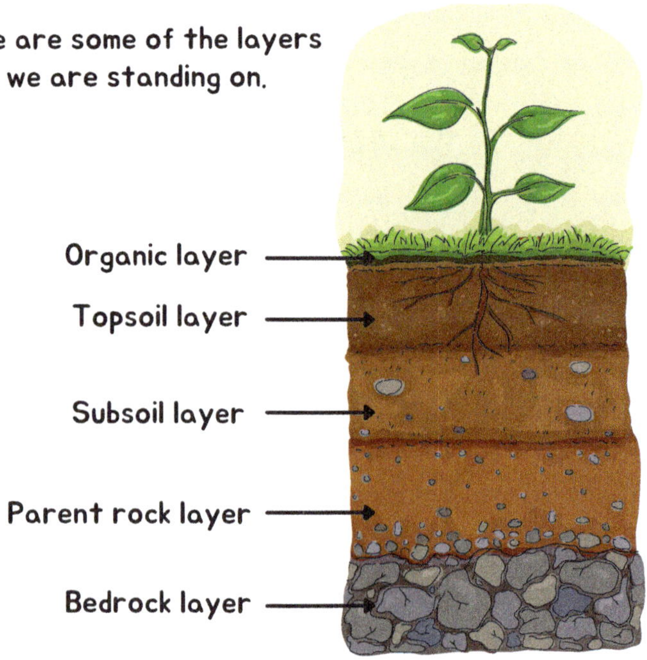

There are different types of soil with different properties because of the different types of rock which they are on.

Cover up the page before with a sheet of paper and label this diagram from memory.

How did you do?

Remember learning is a fun journey! If you didn't get them all correct yet, that is ok because you can try again later.

Keep learning, keep practicing and keep growing!

Learn about different...

Soil

...and which plants love each type

Clay Soil

Clay soil usually feels sticky and thick because it drains poorly so stays wet. If it becomes dry, clay soil has a very hard texture. Plants grow well in clay soil if it is well drained because it holds more nutrients than other soils.

Plants which love clay soil:

Aster (type of perennial)
Bergamot (type of perennial)
Weigela (type of shrub)

Perennial means a plant which gives flowers every year

Sandy Soil

Sandy soil is very grainy and feels gritty. It is a well draining soil so some nutrients are washed through it which can make sandy soil low in nutrients (sometimes it is called "hungry" soil).

Plants which love sandy soil:

Tulip (type of bulb)
Sun rose (type of shrub)
Hibiscus (type of shrub)

Silty Soil

Silty soil has a smooth texture and is a well drained soil. The soil keeps moisture and is more fertile (has more nutrients). This soil is also easier to handle than sandy soil as it holds its shape better.

Plants which love silty soil:

Mahonia (type of shrub)
Ornamental vine (type of climber)
Hakonechloa (type of grass)

Peaty Soil

Peaty soil is very dark in colour and is acidic so it can be low in nutrients. But peaty soil can produce amazing plant growth if you add fertiliser. This soil contains a higher amount of peat (organic matter) hence its name of peaty soil.

Plants which love peaty soil:

Heather
Witch hazel
Rhododendron
These are all a type of shrub

Loamy Soil

Loamy soil is sometimes called the "perfect" soil. This is because it has good properties such as holding enough moisture but it drains well, it is full of nutrients so plants grow well and it does not dry out in the summer.

Plants which love loamy soil:

Wisteria (type of climber)
Rubus (type of shrub)
Delphinium (type of perennial)

Exploring soils around you

Explore the different types of soil in your garden or at the park.

Describe how it looks (e.g. stony, grainy, hard, wet), the colour (e.g. light brown, tar-like, sandy colour), the texture of how it feels (e.g. gritty, sticky, dry) and think about what plants you want to grow.

A world of...

Mini beasts

...living in the soil. Let's have a look!

There is a whole other world right under out feet!
These are the mini beasts!

These tiny creatures are really fascinating because they can do amazing things. For example, a species of the Horned Dung Beetle can pull 1,141 times its body weight!

Spot the Worm

How many worms can you see?
Some maybe long so have a good look!

Number of Worms:

____

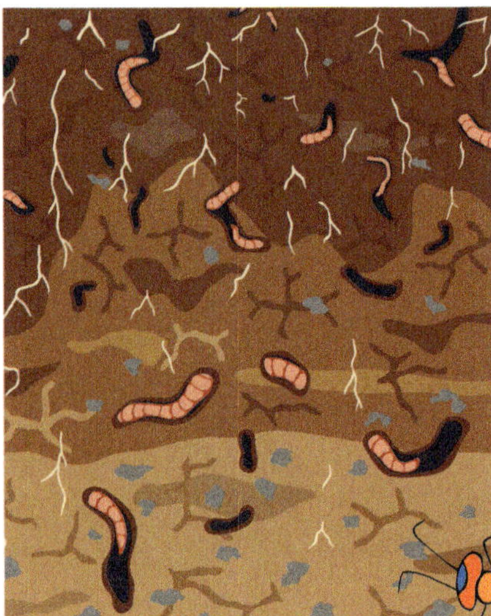

Name the Mini beast & match the fact

Write the name of each minibeast in the box and draw a line to match the amazing fact to the correct insect.

1 [ ]

Ⓐ This minibeast has 14 legs and an exoskeleton.

2 [ ]

Ⓑ This minibeast has no lungs. Instead it breaths through its skin.

3 [ ]

Ⓒ This minibeast can reach a top speed of half an inch per second.

4 [ ]

Ⓓ This minibeast has 2 stomachs and can swim.

1=C, 2=A, 3=D, 4=B

How to make...

Compost

...in your back garden in 5 easy to follow steps

Compost is a mixture of recycled natural things like vegetable waste and decayed plants. Compost has extra nutrients than usual soil because it has the minerals from all the decayed ingredients.

You will need:

- Small compost bin with lid
- Compostable contents (like scrunched up paper, tea bags, vegetable waste, straw)
- Gardening fork

1. Make some holes carefully in the base of the compost bin.
2. Place it near or on bare soil so that worms can wriggle into it.
3. Start putting your compostable contents straight into it.
4. Now wait...every month use the gardening fork to turn over the contents of your compost bin. This is to let in air and the more you turn it, the quicker your compost will make.
5. It takes from 6-24 months to make compost. It will have a dark colour, crumbly texture and be a rich compost when ready.

Compostable contents

Here is a helpful list of stuff which can and can not be tossed into your compost bin.

✓	✗
Raw fruit or vegetable chopping or peelings	Wood twigs
Grass cuttings	Dog or cat poo
Dead plants and leaves	Meat or cooked food scraps
Tea leaves and coffee ground	Bones
Scrunched up newspaper	Perennial weed roots
	Plants with illness

Chapter 8

You & Nature

To walk in nature
is to witness
a thousand
miracles

Mary Davis

Nature game...

Who am I?

...play and discover yourself too

Connecting with nature will have helped you to connect with your inner self.

Take a moment to describe yourself. Use lots of adjectives and positive words. Celebrate and love who you are because you are unique and nobody else in this world is YOU!

KNOW
WHO
YOU
ARE

This is a multiplayer game. One player has to describe the picture on the card without saying exactly what it is. The other player(s) must guess and name what is on the card.

While outside write a...

Seasons Poem

...the acrostic way

Poetry is a beautiful way to express your ideas, thoughts and feelings. A type of poem which you could write is an acrostic poem. Think of these seasons and use the first letter to think of a word of sentence which helps to describe that season.

W

I

N

T

E

R

S

U

M

M

E

R

Draw or paint a picture of what you have written about to describe each season.

Nature bingo...

Detective Bingo

...can you find 5 in a row?

Take this book with you on your next nature walk. Mark on the Bingo grid when you spot an item on the grid.

You could play against a friend or family member and see who scores a BINGO first!

Try this fun flowers and leaves bingo game. Mark on the Bingo grid when you spot each item.

Play against a friend or family member and see who scores a BINGO first!

You are good at this! Try making your own bingo game with a different theme. Perhaps you could make one for things to spot when you go on your next picnic or when you go camping.

Write you own...

Recount

...describe your connection with nature

Now that you have read this book and done the activities, write a recount to describe the journey you have taken through nature. Think of some fun times you have had in the great outdoors and write about them. Use lots of describing words and include your feelings. Remember to write about things you saw, heard and touched. Take your time and enjoy writing your reflection.

CERTIFICATE OF ACHIEVEMENT

A KIDS VIEW ON NATURE AWARDS

for completing their Nature Journey

Onkaar
Author

Avneet
Author

Printed in Great Britain
by Amazon

72774478R00068